10 Advanced Techniques
That will make you Pro of
Amazon Advertising

Let's explore the proven strategies and tactics, and empower sellers with practical knowledge to excel in Amazon Advertising

MAIMOONA J. IQBAL

Dedication

This book is born out of the love and faith of my parents, who have gifted me the strength to chase my dreams.

To my siblings, my first friends and lifelong companions on this journey, thank you for always standing by my side.

To my loving beautiful husband, whose love inspires me daily to strive for greatness.

And to everyone who has touched this project, your belief and contributions have breathed life into these pages, and for that, I am eternally grateful.

This book is as much yours as it is mine.

CONTENTS

WELCOME TO MY FELLOW SELLERS!

You are reading these top 10 techniques to Amazon Advertising because you are either considering scaling up your Amazon Ads campaigns or seeking tips as a startup entrepreneur to enhance your advertising skills. Fortunately, this resource caters to both scenarios, sharing simple but effective options that are readily available in your campaign manager of adversing console .

I want to emphasize that I'm not advocating for spending excessive amounts of money on Amazon PPC campaigns. On the contrary, this ebook will equip you with the knowledge to independently assess whether PPC campaigns align with your Amazon business goals. For those already familiar with the power of PPC, you will gain valuable skills to establish more cost-effective and optimized campaigns.

If the idea of "paid advertising" makes you apprehensive, hear me out. There are strategies available to suit any budget, and compelling evidence supports the potential benefits of giving PPC a chance to boost your Amazon selling business.

If you are new to PPC, don't worry. You will find glossary at the end of this book and helpful tips to familiarize yourself with key concepts and terminology. I'll also write a separate ebook, that will cover a comprehensive step by step guide from setting up campaigns, right through to managing them and analyzing the report data.

Marketing and advertising are integral parts of running a business and generating profits. Let's explore how we can utilize Amazon PPC for the greater good and enhance our future profitability.

I hope you get lots out of this ebook. If you have any questions or feedback, just drop us a line at support@uprisox.com

What is Amazon Advertising?

Amazon Ads refers to the advertising services and platform provided by Amazon, one of the world's largest online marketplaces. Amazon Ads offers a range of products and information to help you achieve your advertising goals, for registered sellers, vendors, book vendors, Kindle Direct Publishing (KDP) authors, app developers, and/or agencies.

By utilizing Amazon Ads for advertising purposes, you can effectively connect with customers at various stages of their journey. Amazon advertising solutions are designed to align with your specific advertising objectives while simultaneously aiding customers in finding the products they desire. Amazon Ads offers the following products:

Sponsored Products

Cost-per-click ads for individual product listings appear in shopping results and on product detail pages.

Sponsored Brands

Brand ads in shopping results offer self-service, cost-per-click options with a custom headline, logo, and multiple products.

Sponsored Display

Self-service display ads utilize auto-generated creatives and target audiences based on relevant Amazon shopping interests.

Stores

Free, multi-page brand destinations on Amazon showcase your product portfolio and facilitate brand storytelling.

What is Amazon Advertising?

Audio Ads

Ads play on Amazon Music's free tier across Alexa devices, mobile, and desktop.

Video Ads

Streaming TV ads air on connected TVs, publisher channels, networks, IMDb, and IMDb TV. Out-stream video ads display off and on Amazon, excluding video content.

Custom Advertising

Tailor-made advertising experiences are developed in collaboration with Amazon Ads account executives.

Amazon DSP

Amazon's demand side platform allows advertisers to programmatically buy display, video, and audio ads.

Amazon Attribution

This product evaluates the impact of non-Amazon ads media on driving results within Amazon.

1

Set your clear advertising goals

To begin, it is important to establish customized advertising goals aligned with your desired outcomes.

Uncertain about how to begin?
Discover prevalent goals, their corresponding objectives, and essential metrics for measuring success.

GOAL SETTING:

	GOAL	OBJECTIVE	KPIs
AWARENESS	"I aim to enhance brand awareness among a larger audience." "My goal is to expand my customer base by reaching new potential clients." "I aspire to effectively communicate my brand story to a wider audience."	Share the narrative of your brand, connect with prospective customers, and foster trust and confidence in your brand. Optimize your reach to maximize the size of your target audience.	• Impressions • Brand recall lift
CONSIDERATION	"My goal is to increase the likelihood of shoppers considering my product/brand alongside similar brands or products when they browse."	Engage shoppers in a buying mindset through relevant and captivating advertisements. Consideration campaigns are designed to captivate potential customers.	• Traffic • Store visits • Ad engagement • Video views • Email list sign-ups • Detail page visits
CONVERSION	"I aim to boost sales for my products or services." "My goal is to capture the attention of highly interested shoppers and guide them towards making a purchase."	Interact with motivated shoppers who are transitioning from the consideration stage to making a purchase.	• Sales • Return on ad spend • Advertising cost of sales
RETENTION	"I strive to foster loyalty among my existing customers for my product or brand."	Assist in generating repeat sales from customers who have previously purchased your products or services.	• Repeat purchases • Referrals • Store visits • Subscribe & Save

2 Begin with Sponsored Product Ads

Whether you're new or seasoned to Amazon Ads and registered as a seller or vendor on Amazon, I suggest starting with **sponsored product ads.** These ad solutions are user-friendly, compatible with various budget levels, and operate on a cost-per-click model, meaning you only pay when a shopper clicks on your ad. When setting up a sponsored ads campaign, you have the flexibility to choose your budget and bid amount per click. If you're interested in advertising products or services that are not sold on Amazon, you can choose display ads, video ads, and custom ads.

+50% increase in units ordered
ASINs saw an average weekly +50% lift in units ordered within the first year after launching a Sponsored Products campaign.

+30% increase in glance views
ASINs saw an average weekly +30% lift in glance views within the first year after launching a Sponsored Products campaign.

55x

55x increase in impressions
Adding 3 or more bullet points to your product page and advertising with Sponsored Products can help you increase impressions by 55x

93x

93x more unit sales
Adding A+ content to your detail page and advertising with Sponsored Products can help generate up to 93x more unit sales.

Source: https://advertising.amazon.com/solutions/products/sponsored-products/?ref_=a20m_us_search_title

2

Begin with Sponsored Product Ads

Increase Organic sales with Amazon Ads

ROI is a critical factor in Amazon PPC campaigns, but its impact goes beyond direct sales from ads. Interestingly, running successful PPC campaigns can result in a general increase in overall sales.

Consider this scenario: Let's say you invest $500 in a PPC campaign and generate 50 direct sales from those ads. However, during the same month, you notice a significant increase of 150 organic sales compared to your average monthly sales. This represents a remarkable 100% surge in organic sales for that specific product.

Looking at it this way, your PPC campaigns have contributed to an additional 125 sales in a single month. While not all of these sales can be directly attributed to PPC, it's reasonable to conclude that PPC has played a role in boosting your overall revenue. It's worth noting that an increase in PPC sales positively affects your Best Sellers Rank (BSR), which in turn enhances organic sales.

How to Find Out Your Organic Sales and Ad Sales Figures Separately?

Determining the specific figures for organic sales and ad sales separately can be challenging within Amazon Seller Central, as there is no filter option available in campaign manager. Despite various discussions on the Seller Central forum regarding this topic, there is no dedicated tool or report available that can precisely differentiate between sales generated from advertisements and sales generated organically on Amazon. However, you can differentiate the data be following the manual process:

Begin with Sponsored Product Ads

Manual Process

1. Go to Business Reports, check total number of units from there by setting up the time period in which you want to check:

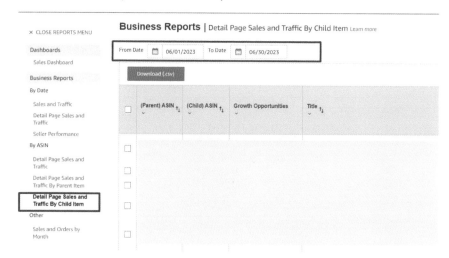

2. Click on "detail Page Sales and Traffic By Child Item" and check the relevant ASIN box that you wish to see the "Units Ordered" i.e 273

3. Now go to campaign manager and filter the relevant ASIN by date range and see the total orders i.e 172. So here you have 101 orders from organic sale.

③ Product listing recommendations

If you look at Campaign Manager in Advertising console, sellers now have the opportunity to discover listing improvements that can enhance the performance of their products. Amazon provides valuable suggestions for potential listing enhancements within the ad groups of existing Sponsored Products campaigns. For example, these recommendations may include adding additional bullet points or product images to an ASIN in order to provide shoppers with more comprehensive information and facilitate informed purchase decisions.

Why this is important for you?

Sellers can now access detailed insights on improving the ASINs within their ad campaigns directly through the ad console. These tailored recommendations address specific products and focus on adding critical missing information, such as descriptions and product search keywords. Implementing these recommendations can significantly increase the likelihood of customers clicking on and engaging with your advertised products.

③ Product listing recommendations

Here are some of the recommendations you may come across for your products within the Campaign Manager:

1. **Create a captivating product title:** Craft an informative and easy-to-read title that quickly communicates key details about your product. We recommend titles between 25 and 200 characters, with an ideal length of around 60 characters.

2. **Showcase at least 4 images:** Including 4 or more high-quality images on your product detail page can enhance sales and drive clicks.

3. **Feature zoomable images:** Enable shoppers to examine your product from different angles and highlight important details by ensuring that your images are at least 1000 pixels in height or width, allowing them to zoom in for a closer look.

4. **Enhance your detail page with A+ content:** If you are enrolled in the Amazon Brand Registry, take advantage of A+ content to describe your product features using enhanced images, strategically placed text, and engaging stories.

5. **Add relevant search terms for your product:** Enhance discoverability by including search terms that shoppers are likely to use when looking for your product.

6. **Provide a detailed and helpful product description:** Utilize the product description to go beyond the basic features outlined in the bullet points and convey the benefits, uses, and value proposition of your product in a concise yet engaging manner.

7. **Incorporate at least 3 bullet points on your detail page:** Use bullet points to provide a clear overview of your product's key features, including details such as contents, uses, dimensions, operational considerations, age rating, skill level, and country of origin.

4
Creative and Free Advertising Strategies

How Free advertising works On and Off Amazon?

Free advertising is a cost-efficient approach that allows brands and businesses to reach their target audiences creatively and resourcefully. Regardless of the size of your company, free marketing can enhance your strategy and expand your brand without expensive campaigns or paid promotions.

To advertise for free, it requires experimentation and hard work. While it may not be the easiest form of advertising, it offers small businesses an opportunity to get started without a large marketing budget. Social media, email promotions, word-of-mouth, and User generated Content (UGC) are just a few ways to promote your business of Amazon and without any cost.

Amazon provides following free services to showcase your products to wider audience.

Amazon Posts

Amazon Posts is an exclusive free program offered to brand-registered sellers, enabling them to share engaging brand and product content through a dynamic "feed" resembling popular social media platforms. With Amazon Posts, brands can seamlessly replicate their existing strategies on platforms like Instagram, creating a cohesive visual experience for customers within the Amazon Marketplace.

Creative and Free Advertising Strategies

Amazon Live

You can discover and explore all live streams on Amazon.com/Live, the platform dedicated to shoppers. When you utilize the Amazon Live Creator app to livestream, there is a chance for your livestream to be featured on Amazon.com/Live. Enjoy the freedom of streaming for free across multiple placements where Amazon shoppers browse.

Amazon Live Creator
Livestream on Amazon.com   **OPEN**
★★★★☆ 27

Creative and Free Advertising Strategies

Amazon Stores

An Amazon Store is a personalized, multi-page shopping destination designed for professional sellers having Brand Registry to showcase their unique brand story and product offerings. Brands can create their own dedicated brand store with multiple versions suits to different holiday events on Amazon without any additional cost, complete with a distinctive Amazon URL.

How to Optimise your Store:

Make sure your customers find you with your Store's custom URL. Usually a long URL is automatically generated once your store is live. You can submit a request to seller support team by sharing a long URL and custom URL you would like to have.

Brand's byline helps in getting organic traffic to your store . It is hyperlinked brand name on product detail page. Make sure it is properly setup and it appears in blue colour under the title of product detail page.

Organic/free marketing as discussed above can also optimise your store by redirecting traffic to your storefront.

Amazon Attribution

To evaluate the effectiveness of your organic marketing endeavors in boosting brand visibility and product discovery on Amazon, you can also leverage a free beta measurement solution known as Amazon Attribution. By utilizing the measurement console provided by Amazon Attribution, you gain valuable insights and metrics to assess the impact and resonance of your cross-channel campaigns on your target audience, ultimately driving your business objectives.

5

Sponsored Brands

Understanding the Potential of Sponsored Brands

Sponsored Brands provide an invaluable opportunity for sellers to elevate their advertising strategies. If you're a professional seller enrolled in Amazon Brand Registry, a vendor, a book vendor, or an agency, Sponsored Brands can be a powerful tool for maximizing your brand's impact.

Sponsored Brands offer a customizable advertising solution designed to captivate your audience. With the ability to showcase your brand logo, a custom headline, and multiple products, these ads hold a prominent position within shopping results and product detail pages. This prime placement significantly boosts brand visibility and drives discovery among customers actively seeking products similar to yours.

Below top of shopping results

Within shopping results

Product detail pages*

Sponsored Brands video ad format*

Source: https://advertising.amazon.com/library/guides/sponsored-brands-what-to-know?ref_=a20m_us_p_sb_lbr_jg_sbcmpltgd#04

5 Sponsored Brands

Let's delve into the key features that make Sponsored Brands a game-changer:

1. **Goal:** Amplify brand awareness, drive consideration, spur acquisition, foster loyalty.
2. **Targeting:** Precisely target your audience based on keywords, categories, or specific products.
3. **Reach:** Seamlessly connect with your target customers directly on Amazon.
4. **Placement:** Secure prominent ad placement within shopping results and product detail pages, ensuring maximum visibility.
5. **Ad Formats:** Choose from various ad formats, such as product collections, Store spotlights (where available), and captivating videos (where available).
6. **Destination Options:** Drive traffic to product detail pages, create new landing pages, direct customers to your Store, or even use custom URLs for tailored experiences.
7. **Creative Freedom:** Enjoy full control over your ad creatives, customizing them with product or lifestyle images and captivating videos (where available).
8. **Cost Structure:** Pay only for clicks with the cost-per-click model, while setting a daily budget to manage your spending effectively.
9. **Eligibility:** Sellers enrolled in Amazon Brand Registry and vendors can take full advantage of Sponsored Brands.

Effective Targeting Strategies

For optimal reach and coverage, utilize both keyword targeting and product targeting in your advertising strategy. Note that you can only choose one targeting type per campaign. By combining these approaches, you can effectively connect with your desired audience and maximize the success of your Sponsored Brands campaigns.

Sponsored Display Ads

Reaching Relevant Audiences Effortlessly

Sponsored Display is a versatile advertising solution suitable for businesses of all sizes and budgets, regardless of whether they sell on Amazon. It empowers advertisers to effortlessly discover and connect with relevant audiences. By tailoring display advertising campaigns to specific goals, businesses can effectively engage audiences throughout their shopping and entertainment journeys, both within and beyond the Amazon ecosystem. With dynamically optimized creatives, Sponsored Display ensures maximum impact and audience engagement.

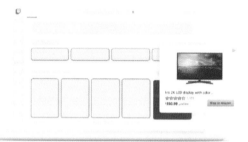

Distinguishing Amazon DSP from Sponsored Display

Sponsored Display and Amazon DSP serve distinct purposes in the realm of advertising:

Sponsored Display: Designed as a self-service display advertising product, Sponsored Display enables advertisers to create and manage their own display campaigns within the Amazon advertising ecosystem. It offers a user-friendly interface, allowing advertisers to target specific audiences and optimize their ad placements effectively.

Amazon DSP: On the other hand, Amazon DSP (Demand-Side Platform) provides a programmatic advertising solution that goes beyond display ads. It allows advertisers to programmatically purchase various types of ads, which include display ads but extend to other formats as well. Amazon DSP offers more advanced features and capabilities, giving advertisers greater control and flexibility in their advertising campaigns.

7 Product Targeting

Product Targeting: Connecting with Relevant Audiences

Product targeting is a powerful feature available in both Sponsored Display and Sponsored Products campaigns. It allows you to strategically place your ads in front of customers who are browsing similar or complementary products on Amazon, driving consideration and boosting sales.

Let's explore the benefits of product targeting in each campaign type:

Sponsored Display

With Sponsored Display, you can inspire customer action through captivating display campaigns. By utilizing product targeting, you can engage audiences who are exploring products and categories similar to yours. The automatically generated creatives showcase deals and savings badges, capturing customers' attention and highlighting relevant offers. Customize your ads with a unique headline and logo to effectively communicate your brand story and product value.

Iris PowerZoom B2100 14.1 MP Digital Camera with Built-In S...
⭐⭐⭐⭐☆ 1,133
$98.88 ✓prime

Savings & Sales

Accent ATHLETICS

Run faster, run lighter.

Save 20%
Accent Athletics Lightweight Breathable Running Shoes
$69.99 ✓prime

Source: https://advertising.amazon.com/blog/reach-relevant-audiences-with-product-targeting/?ref_=a20m_us_search_title

Product Targeting

Sponsored Products

Promote individual product listings with Sponsored Products. Product targeting allows you to reach customers who are actively searching for products like yours. Your ads can appear at the bottom of product detail pages, within relevant categories, or in shopping results, directing customers to your product page for a seamless shopping experience.

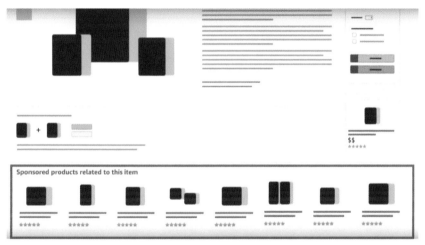

Source: https://advertising.amazon.com/blog/reach-relevant-audiences-with-product-targeting/?ref_=a20m_us_search_title

By leveraging product targeting in both Sponsored Display and Sponsored Products, you can expand your reach and connect with more customers. Drive consideration for your product portfolio with relevant audiences, and convert individual products when shoppers are ready to make a purchase.

Please note that product targeting offers various refinements such as price, star rating, and Prime shipping eligibility, enabling you to fine-tune your campaigns and make your products stand out.

8

Keywords Strategy for Amazon Ads

When customers visit Amazon, they often begin by searching for products using specific keywords or phrases. While organic discovery is possible, advertising with sponsored ads allows you to target customers based on their search queries. By selecting relevant keywords and incorporating them into your sponsored ads campaigns, you can increase the visibility of your products when customers' search queries align with your targeted keywords.

Developing a keyword strategy for your sponsored ads campaigns involves identifying the most effective keywords, organizing them into distinct campaigns aligned with your objectives, and optimizing your strategy to optimize your advertising spend and achieve your desired results. Notably, sellers who consistently ran Sponsored Products campaigns for 12 months experienced an average 11.2% higher return on ad spend (ROAS) compared to the first month.

Keyword targeting is available in two sponsored ads solutions: Sponsored Products and Sponsored Brands.

Discovering Targeted Keywords

To kickstart your keyword strategy for Amazon sponsored ads campaigns, follow these four effective strategies:

Leverage automatic campaigns: Analyze the Search Term Report from your Sponsored Products automatic campaigns to identify top-performing keywords.

Be specific: Utilize keyword combinations that clearly highlight the unique characteristics, materials, or benefits of your products.

Incorporate your brand name: Include your brand's name in keywords to enhance impressions for branded searches and capture the attention of shoppers specifically seeking products from your brand.

Harness organic keywords: Take advantage of keywords already added to your product detail page, as they tend to be highly relevant to your offerings.

By employing these strategies, you can start incorporating targeted keywords into your campaigns.

Keywords Strategy for Amazon Ads

Incorporating Your Keywords

The level of specificity in the keywords you select for manual keyword targeting plays a crucial role. The choice depends on your advertising objectives and desired audience. Consider the following keyword types for your campaigns:

Generic keywords: Broad and less specific terms representing broader categories (e.g., chair or dining chair).

Longtail keywords: More specific phrases with lower search volume but higher relevance (e.g., white wood dining chair).

Branded keywords: Incorporating your brand's name (e.g., Modernata dining chair set) to target customers already familiar with your brand.

Seasonal keywords: Including terms related to specific moments or peak periods during the year (e.g., Valentine's Day table decor).

Grouping keywords based on your advertising goals enables better targeting, bidding, measurement, and budgeting.

In addition to keyword specificity, the keyword match type is crucial in determining how closely the keywords you bid on align with customer shopping queries. There are three options:

Broad match: Least restrictive, providing high potential traffic exposure, suitable for driving awareness and gaining insights into how customers discover your products.

Phrase match: Moderately restrictive, ideal for longtail keyword strategies to drive consideration and conversion.

Exact match: Most precise and restrictive, effective in driving conversions, best used when you have researched high-performing shopping queries.

While there is no specific number of keywords to add, we recommend a minimum of 25 terms. Combine keyword specificity with the appropriate match type to optimize your keyword targeting strategy.

8

Keywords Strategy for Amazon Ads

Optimizing Your Keyword Strategy

Keyword targeting requires ongoing optimization to ensure optimal performance. After running a campaign for approximately two weeks, you'll have enough data to make informed decisions and enhance your keyword strategy.

There are three key ways to optimize your keyword strategy: refining match types, adding new keywords, and incorporating negative keyword targets.

To refine match types, review your campaign manager and identify keywords and match types that yield positive outcomes, such as a high return on ad spend (ROAS) and a low advertising cost of sales (ACOS). If a specific match type is not meeting your desired goal, consider pausing it.

Continuously monitor your Search Term Report to identify high-performing search queries and add them as new keywords using exact match, aligning with your campaign objectives.

When it comes to negative keywords, consider which search queries you don't want your ads to appear against. For example, if you're advertising a luxury product, terms like "cheap" or "inexpensive" may not be relevant. Add these negative keywords, along with any others from your Search Term Report that are not delivering desired results. Employing a negative keyword strategy improves ad relevance, helps manage your budget, and ensures a refined keyword targeting approach.

Analytics and Measuring Performance

The Importance of Advertising Metrics

Advertising metrics play a crucial role in understanding the impact and effectiveness of your marketing efforts. Here are some reasons why these metrics matter:

Measure Success: Advertising metrics provide quantifiable data that helps you assess the success of your campaigns. From upper-funnel metrics like impressions and clicks to more concrete outcomes such as sales, subscriptions, and acquiring new customers, these metrics allow you to gauge the effectiveness of your advertising strategies.

Understanding Your Audiences: Many advertisers struggle with confidently reaching the right audiences. By leveraging the vast amount of first-party insights available across Amazon devices and sites, you can gain a comprehensive understanding of your customers and the audiences your advertising reaches. These insights provide a holistic view, helping you better comprehend your target customers and refine your advertising strategies accordingly.

Proving Advertising Impact: Linking marketing investments to business objectives and results can be a challenge for many marketers. However, with the right advertising metrics, you can demonstrate the impact of your campaigns on sales performance and audience response. Metrics like new-to-brand data, advertising cost of sales (ACOS), and return on ad spend (ROAS) serve as evidence of your advertising's effectiveness and its contribution to driving sales.

Optimizing Your Campaigns: To achieve optimal results, it is essential to combine first- and third-party reporting, giving you a comprehensive view of your campaign outcomes both on and off Amazon. By analyzing these reports, you can identify the most effective tactics and channels, allowing you to optimize your campaigns and develop a well-informed advertising strategy. This data-driven approach ensures that you make the most of your advertising efforts and maximize your return on investment.

⑨ Analytics and Measuring Performance

Improve Decision-Making: By analyzing advertising metrics, you gain valuable insights that inform your decision-making process. Understanding the performance of your ads helps you identify what works and what doesn't, enabling you to optimize your campaigns for better results.

Optimize Campaigns: Robust measurement allows you to identify areas of improvement in your advertising campaigns. By tracking metrics like click-through rates, conversions, and customer acquisition, you can make data-driven adjustments to optimize your campaigns and enhance their overall performance.

Justify Investments: Advertising metrics help you demonstrate the value and impact of your marketing efforts to stakeholders. By showcasing tangible outcomes such as increased sales or customer engagement, you can justify your advertising investments and secure continued support for future campaigns.

Identify Opportunities: By monitoring advertising metrics, you can discover new opportunities and trends. Insights gained from these metrics can highlight areas where you can capitalize on untapped markets, target specific audience segments, or refine your messaging to better resonate with your target customers.

Amazon Measuring Solutions

Amazon Attribution

Amazon Attribution is a dedicated measurement solution designed to track the performance of non-Amazon digital marketing strategies. It provides valuable advertising metrics that go beyond standard traffic data, offering insights into important conversion metrics specific to Amazon, such as detail page views, Add to Carts, and purchases. With Amazon Attribution, advertisers can gain a comprehensive understanding of the impact and effectiveness of their digital marketing efforts, enabling them to make informed decisions and optimize their campaigns for better results.

Analytics and Measuring Performance

Amazon DSP

The reporting in the Amazon DSP provides valuable insights into retail activity on Amazon, allowing you to compare performance before, during, and after your campaigns. Additionally, the campaign reporting highlights the impact of your campaigns on customer behavior, from discovery to research and purchase of your products. You can also access third-party reporting solutions, including brand lift and off-line sales impact, for a comprehensive understanding of your campaign's effectiveness.

Sponsored Brands

With Sponsored Brands, you can access detailed reports that offer insights into your campaign performance, including placement performance, ad clicks, sales, and advertising cost of sales (ACOS). ACOS represents the percentage of ad spend compared to sales. Additionally, Sponsored Brands provides new-to-brand metrics, which measure the purchases made by first-time customers of your brand on Amazon that were a result of your campaign. These metrics help you gauge the effectiveness of your Sponsored Brands campaigns in driving new customer acquisitions.

Sponsored Display

Sponsored Display provides comprehensive reports that include essential advertising metrics such as ACOS (advertising cost of sales), orders, detail page views, and glance views. These metrics offer valuable insights into the performance and impact of your Sponsored Display campaigns, allowing you to track key metrics related to sales, visibility, and customer engagement.

Sponsored Products

Sponsored Products campaign reports offer valuable insights into the sales and performance of your advertised products. These reports provide a comprehensive view of your campaign's performance, including detailed information on sales, performance by keyword, and the effectiveness of different ad placements. By analyzing these reports, you can gain valuable insights to optimize your Sponsored Products campaigns and drive better results for your products.

Get, Set, Ready for key shopping events

Complete your Prime Day tasks with confidence by following these essential tips we've outlined below.

Strategic Approaches and Pro Seller Techniques

Targeting
- In the weeks leading up to Prime Day, diligently monitor your campaigns to identify high-performing keywords and products.
- Employ a multi-ad approach and explore various ad formats to maximize your impact.
- Optimize your event budget by employing astute financial management.
- For a quick start with Sponsored Products, utilize automatic targeting.
- If you're creating Sponsored Brands or Sponsored Display campaigns, consider manual targeting.
- If you possess sufficient data from your reports and have previously run automatic targeting campaigns with Sponsored Products, manual targeting can prove beneficial.
- Experiment with new keywords and expand the scope of your campaigns, while remaining cautious of any restricted keywords.
- Employ a diversified mix of match types to devise a multifaceted strategy. Leverage different targeting tactics such as keyword targeting, product targeting, negative targeting, contextual targeting, and Sponsored Display audiences.

Get, Set, Ready for key shopping events

Bids and Budgeting

- Prepare yourself for a potential surge in traffic.
- Meticulously monitor your bids and budgets throughout Prime Day.
- Shift your budget allocation to your most effective campaigns to maximize returns.
- Leverage insights derived from recent campaigns to adjust your bids strategically.
- Enhance your chances of driving sales by utilizing dynamic bidding strategies.

Driving Brand Growth and Maximising Creativity

- If you haven't already, seize the opportunity to create your Store today, free of charge.
- Utilize captivating videos to inspire and captivate shoppers, stimulating their desire to learn more about your brand and potentially make a purchase.
- Ensure your Store is well-prepared for Prime Day and undergoes the moderation process.
- Utilize custom product imagery as shoppable images within your Store, fostering a strong connection between your audience and your products.

International Advertising

- Consider advertising in countries where you already have a presence or plan to operate during Prime Day.
- Take advantage of regional events that align with key overlapping occasions.
- Acquaint yourself with the diverse array of tools at your disposal to effectively advertise across multiple countries.

Conclusion

Amazon advertising offers a multitude of opportunities for businesses to thrive in the digital marketplace. Throughout the book "10 Advanced Techniques That Will Make You a Pro of Amazon Advertising," we have explored the various aspects and strategies that can empower advertisers to succeed on this platform.

Congratulations on reaching the end of this guide! I appreciate your commitment and hope you found it valuable. Throughout our journey, we have explored the power of Amazon PPC and its positive impact on both sales and organic performance.

Remember, knowledge is power, and having this guide at your fingertips will ensure that you have the necessary tools to navigate the world of Amazon PPC effectively. If you ever find yourself facing challenges or needing additional support, you can always refer back to this resource for guidance.

Thank you for your time and dedication throughout this journey. I hope you gained valuable takeaways and feel more empowered to optimize your Amazon PPC campaigns. Wishing you continued success in your Amazon business ventures!

Please feel free to contact me by emailing maimoona.iqbal@uprisox.com if you have any questions!

Glossary

Throughout this guide, we have encountered various terms and jargon related to Amazon PPC advertising. It is important to familiarize ourselves with these terms to navigate the world of PPC effectively. Here is a comprehensive glossary to help you understand and refer back to these terms whenever needed:

Advertising Cost of Sale (ACoS): A specific Amazon metric that measures the ratio of advertising costs to sales revenue generated by an ad. A lower ACoS indicates more cost-effective ads.

Ad Group: A segment within a campaign used to group related keywords and products for more granular control and bid management.

Bid: The maximum amount you are willing to pay for each click on your ad, which determines its visibility and position.

Campaign: A logical grouping of products, keywords, or match types in your advertising strategy, allowing you to set targeting and budget parameters.

Click: When a shopper interacts with your sponsored ad by clicking on it. You pay for each click, regardless of whether a purchase is made.

Click-Through Rate (CTR): The percentage of ad clicks divided by the total number of ad impressions. It provides insights into the effectiveness of your ads and can vary depending on campaign targeting and match types.

Conversion: When a shopper clicks on your ad and completes a desired action, such as making a purchase. Conversions can be measured immediately or within a specified timeframe.

Conversion Rate: The percentage of ad clicks that result in a conversion, calculated by dividing the number of conversions by the number of clicks.

Cost Per Click (CPC): The average cost you pay for each click on your ad, providing insights into your average advertising spend.

Detail Page Views (DPV): This indicates how many people viewed your product detail page after clicking on your ad.

Cost per Acquisition (CPA): This calculates how much it costs for you to acquire a customer.

Order Rate: The percentage of clicks that lead to a sale.

Glossary

Cost Per Sale (CPS): The average amount spent to generate a sale, indicating the cost-effectiveness of your advertising efforts.

Default Bid: The default bid amount set at the ad group level, applied to all keywords within that group unless specified otherwise.

Impressions: The number of times your ad is shown to shoppers, regardless of whether they interact with it.

Keywords: Terms or phrases you bid on and compete for, representing the words shoppers use when searching on Amazon.

Match Types: Categories that define how closely the keywords you bid on must match shoppers' search terms. These include broad, phrase, and exact match.

Broad Match: With broad match, your ad will be triggered by a wide range of search terms that include synonyms, variations, and plurals of your keyword. This match type generates the highest number of impressions because it allows for more variance in the search terms. However, it may also lead to less precise targeting.

Phrase Match: In phrase match, your ad will be triggered when the search term includes your keyword phrase in the correct order. Additional words can appear before or after the phrase, allowing for variations, plurals, abbreviations, and acronyms. This match type offers a more focused targeting approach compared to broad match, as it narrows down the searches that can trigger your ad

Exact Match: Exact match requires the search term to exactly match your keyword. The only allowed variants are misspellings, singulars, and plurals. This match type provides the most targeted approach, resulting in lower costs per click and reduced wastage. However, it also means that your ad will have fewer impressions, as there are fewer variations of the exact keyword.

Bounce Rate: The percentage of users who click your ad, but leave without making a purchase.

Average Order Value (AOV): The average value of each order placed. This helps in understanding the profit potential of your campaigns.

Glossary

Product Ad: An ad showcasing your product on the Amazon website, promoting visibility and sales.

Sales Revenue: The total revenue generated from sales directly attributed to your sponsored ads.

Search Terms: The specific keywords or phrases used by shoppers when searching for products on Amazon.

Suggested Bid: A guideline provided by Amazon to help set your maximum bid amount for winning ad auctions.

Targeting Type: The method chosen for targeting your ads, either automatic or manual. Automatic targeting uses product listings to determine targeting, while manual targeting allows for more control and customization.

Advertising Creative: Advertising creative refers to the visual and textual elements, including imagery, videos, and text, that are used to convey your message to your target audience in an advertisement.

Advertising Format: Advertising format refers to the specific type or style of advertisement that is utilized, such as video ads or display ads, to effectively deliver your message to the audience.

Advertising Objective: Advertising objective represents the specific goal or outcome you aim to achieve through your digital advertising efforts. This can include objectives like increasing brand awareness, driving consideration, promoting purchases, or building customer loyalty.

Advertising Placement: Advertising placement refers to the specific locations or platforms where your advertisements are displayed. This can include appearing in shopping queries on the Amazon website, on Amazon devices like Fire TV or Fire tablets, or on third-party websites.

Audio Ads: Audio ads are advertisements that are played during audio content, such as streaming music, digital radio, and podcasts, allowing you to reach and engage with audiences through audio channels.

Lifetime Value (LTV): This measures the projected revenue that a customer will generate during their lifetime.

Glossary

Custom Advertising Solutions: Custom advertising solutions involve creating tailored advertising campaigns that go beyond standard ad products. Amazon Ads offers custom solutions like home page takeovers, Fire TV placements, customized destination pages, and even non-digital formats such as on-box advertising and in-store displays.

Display Ads: Display ads are visual advertisements that appear on websites and combine text and visual elements to convey a message. They typically include a call-to-action (CTA) that directs users to a landing page for further engagement.

Managed vs. Self-Service: In digital advertising, products are often categorized as either self-service or managed. Self-service products like Sponsored Brands and Sponsored Display allow advertisers and agencies to directly create and manage their campaigns, while managed services like Streaming TV ads and custom advertising solutions require varying levels of support from Amazon Ads.

Sponsored Ads: Sponsored ads are a suite of self-service ad products offered by Amazon Ads. They include Sponsored Products, Sponsored Brands, and Sponsored Display, which enable advertisers to promote their products and brands across Amazon's ecosystem.

Video Ads: Video ads refer to online advertisements that incorporate videos as the primary content. This can include in-stream and out-stream video ads on browsers and apps, allowing advertisers to deliver engaging video content to their target audience. Streaming TV ads specifically target audiences consuming streaming content through various platforms.

New-to-brand metrics: provide advertisers with visibility into whether a purchase, attributed to an ad, was made by a new customer or an existing customer of the brand's product on Amazon within a one-year timeframe.

ROAS: or Return on Advertising Spend, is a metric that measures the revenue generated from an advertising campaign relative to the amount spent on ads. It helps evaluate the profitability and effectiveness of marketing efforts. A higher ROAS indicates a more successful campaign in terms of generating revenue.

Glossary

TACoS: or Total Advertising Cost of Sales, is a metric that measures the advertising cost as a percentage of total sales. It helps assess the efficiency and profitability of Amazon advertising campaigns. A lower TACoS indicates a more cost-effective campaign.

Gross Profit: It is calculated as sales minus the cost of goods sold (COGS) minus advertising costs. This will give you an idea of the profitability of your campaigns.

Post-Click Conversion Rate: The percentage of clicks that result in an eventual conversion, even if it doesn't happen immediately after the click.

Brand Lift: This measures the increase in interactions with your brand as a result of your ad. Interactions might include increased searches for your brand or more purchases of your products.

Customer Retention Rate: The percentage of customers who make another purchase from your brand after the initial purchase.

Bonuses

Helium 10

Boost your business with H10 Amazon FBA and Walmart seller software. Drive results, maximize efficiency, and stay ahead of the competition.

20% Off · SCAN ME

JungleScout

Jungle Scout is an American company providing SaaS-based tool for search and market analytics, inventory management and sales intelligence for companies selling on online marketplaces.

35% Off · SCAN ME

SELLERBOARD

Automate Email Follow Up Campaigns for Reviews and Feedback. Boost PPC Advertising. Analyze FBA Profit. Manage Inventory. Get Refunded for Lost & Damaged Items.

FREE 2 Months · SCAN ME

Bonuses

ÜPRISOX

I am offering a complimentary PPC audit for Amazon Sellers. Take advantage of this opportunity and scan the link for more information.

SCAN ME

 # Chat with Telegram Personal AI Assistant

Your AI-powered assistant is equipped to search through our extensive library of resources to provide you the answers you need.

SCAN ME

ONE LAST THING...

Thank you so much for reading this book. I poured a lot of sweat and tears into it.

Could I ask a teeny-weeny favor? Please could you leave a review for this book on Amazon? Whether you thought it was the coolest thing ever, not quite your cup of hot chocolate, or somewhere in between, I'd love to have your feedback.

Your review is a shining star for an author like me, guiding more readers towards my book. And guess what? You, my amazing reader, can help make that happen!

Big thanks in advance! It's like you're my personal superhero!

Maimoona J. Iqbal

Printed in Great Britain
by Amazon

32045904R00023